My Love Letter to God

POEMS BY
MICHELE FOWLER

Written Words Publishing LLC
14189 E Dickinson Drive, Unit F
Aurora, CO 80014
www.writtenwordspublishing.com

Published by Written Words Publishing LLC March 3, 2023

ISBN: 979-8-9873088-3-7 (paperback)
ISBN: 979-8-9873088-4-4 (eBook)

Library of Congress Control Number: 2023903939

Cover designed by Written Words Publishing LLC

Manufactured and printed in the United States of America

CONTENTS

SELF-LOVE

Self-love, self-care, she is me
Broken and damaged, not loving me
Hurt and confused
One day, I met You
You pick me up by my crown and told me, "Darling, smile"
You showed me love
Not knowing I could be forgiven and set free
You broke these chains that held me

She is me, a daughter of a King
You give me strength
You give me life
You stand me high above all things
You remind me to keep going
*"For I know the plans I have for you,' declares the LORD, 'plans to
    prosper you and not to harm you, plans to give you hope and a
    future"* (Jeremiah 29:11).

Self-love, self-care
I'm working on me!

SHEKINAH GLORY

As she smiles, the sun beams on her
God can't help but shine His shekinah glory on her
When she walks in the room, all the people can't stop but
        stare
She's a gift from above
She's timeless
She's ageless
She is more precious than jewels, and nothing you desire can
        compare with her

Just as water reflects the face, so the heart reflects the
        person
Long life is in her right hand
In her left hand are riches and honor
Her ways are ways of pleasantness and all her paths are
        peace
She is a tree of life to those who lay hold of her
Those who hold her fast are called blessed

Shekinah glory rain down on her

DAUGHTER OF ZION

Stand tall Daughter of Zion
Don't you know daughter you're under the special regard of
      the Father
Behold and take joy
You are altogether beautiful my love
There is no flaw in you
He will cover you with His pinions
And under His wings you may seek refuge
His faithfulness is a shield and bulwark
He watches over you day and night
I will restore the fortunes of my people Israel they shall
      rebuild the ruined cities and inhabit them
They shall plant vineyards and drink their wine
They shall make gardens and eat their fruit
I will plant them on their land
They shall never again be uprooted out of the land that I
      have given them says the Lord your God

ALABASTER BOX

Earnestly I seek You; I thirst for You
My whole being longs for You
In a dry and parched land where there is no water
Ask and it will be given to you
Seek and you will find
Knock and the door will be opened to you
Jesus, I come humble to You
As I bow down to You and touch the hem of Your garment
As the lady of the issue of blood my pain stops
She felt such pain, some spoke in anger
But yet she pressed a way
She cried like Mary at Your feet with her alabaster box
With no words said
You still heard every word that was on her heart
The blood You shed for her overflows over her
She is healed

DEAR GOD, IT'S ME YOUR DAUGHTER

Dear God, it's me again Your daughter

I come to You humble asking for You to light my path

For who is God save the Lord or who is a rock save our
      God

It is God that girdeth me with strength, and maketh my way
      perfect

He maketh my feet like hinds' feet, and setteth me upon my
      high places

He teacheth my hands to war, so that a bow of steel is
      broken by mine arms

Thou hast also given me the shield of thy salvation and thy
      right hand hath holden me up, and thy gentleness
      hath made me great

Dear God, I am Your daughter

IT'S YOUR SWEET FRAGRANCE

It's Your sweet fragrance around me
That draws me close to You
Your beauty is like the olive tree
Your fragrance like the cedars of Lebanon
Born a son of a virgin, You came to die for me
How can someone love me
Hurt and abused, broken and scorned flesh turn apart
How can someone lay down their life so I can be me
You speak to the storms in my life and they shall vanish
If I'm dispersed in the uttermost parts of the world, You
    will gather and fetch me
You wrap me in Your gentle loving arms and tell me, "My
    child, you are mine"
It's Your sweet fragrance around me that draws me close to
    You

ANOTHER LOVE STORY

Another love story how a young girl fell in love with You
Drowning in my sorrow, losing hope of life
I was the girl that cried out in distress for You
Mislead, misunderstood, took advantage of
My God, why me
Living in depression with no escape out, my mind was
        bound to the sin that held me
When I think of the women that cried out to You, Ruth was
        born into a life of destruction all around her and You
        captured her and set her free
The goodness of Your love overflows for me
There's a greater purpose in me
I'm living proof that God is within me
This is not just another love story
This is me at my wailing well crying out to You
Your endless love and Your gentle loving arms
Never out fails me
I'm never alone, You walk beside me
Another love story on how You love me

VIRTUOUS WOMAN

Her soul is calm as an ocean
Her eyes sparkle with dreams
Her name is from heaven
She's the sweetest woman you'll ever meet
When she speaks, she has the law of kindness on her lips
She's not the woman you take for granted
She's a virtuous woman
She considereth a field and buyeth it
With the fruit of her hands, she planteth a vineyard
She stretcheth out her hand to the poor
She reacheth forth her hands to the needy
Strength and honour are her clothing
She shall rejoice in time to come
Give her of the fruit of her hands and let her own works
        praise her in the gates
She is a virtuous woman

STRENGTH IS WITHIN ME

Strength is me
A strong woman
Clothed in dignity
Intelligent I am
She can be whatever she wants to be
She speaks for the injustice
She's not afraid to stand ten toes
She's a fighter who fights for what she believes
A strong female lead
In this world, they say a woman can't have rights to believe
She's an advocate for the women who can't speak
She marches for what is right
Moving the old out with the new
Courage is she
Determined to help every woman believe
Strength is within me

LAUGHTER BEHIND PAIN

Laughter is behind her pain
She smiles to keep a warm embrace
Deep down inside is scars that's within her
A fighter she is
Someone that will not be broken
She's a woman that stands on pride
Someone that will find peace
She will not be troubled
Writing is her passion
Writing to touch hearts of others
Hoping someday they'll hear the words she's saying
A phenomenal woman she is
Beyond her scars she is something great

SINKING DOWN SHORE

Weather my life was in destruction
Sinking down shore
Past trauma that I went through
Living deep into depression
My life was sailing away
Blaming myself for what happened to me
Insecurities and problems that followed me
Am I beautiful
Am I enough
I was drowning in sorrow
Not knowing how to express myself
I was drowning in this upmist rain
I know I love God, how much more pain
I was angry with myself and God
Why I had to go through this pain
God whispered to me and told me
You're here to change the world
The rain is only here to plant your seed

UNSPOKEN WORDS

Being a woman is tough
Every day is a challenge we face
Many unspoken words
Being a student trying to make a career
Being a mother bringing light into this world
Some women can bare childhood, some don't
Being a doctor trying to save lives
Being a single mother trying to take care of her babies
Living in depression due to trauma
It's a lot on a woman's shoulders
Although her shoulders are heavy, she will never go weak
She has integrity to have the strength to keep pushing
Being a woman doesn't come easy

I DANCE UNTO YOU PSALMS 150

When I think of the goodness of Your name, I dance unto
       You
Rejoicing, shouting, singing
My heart will sing Your praises and not be silent
Praise the LORD, praise God in His sanctuary
Praise Him in His mighty heavens
Praise Him for His acts of power
Praise Him for His surpassing greatness
Praise Him with the sounding of the trumpet
Praise Him with the harp and lyre
Praise Him with timbrel and dancing
Praise Him with the strings and pipe
Praise Him with the clash of cymbals
Praise Him with resounding cymbals
Let everything that has breath praise the LORD
Praise the LORD

THE LORD IS MY PROTECTOR

The Lord Is My Refuge who shall I fear
Thou hast delivered me from the strivings of the people
Thou hast made me the head of the heathen
People whom I have not known shall serve me
As soon as they hear of me, they shall obey me
The strangers shall submit themselves unto me
The strangers shall fade away and be afraid out of their close
    places
The Lord liveth and blessed be my rock
Let the God of my salvation be exalted
It is God that avengeth me and subdueth the people under
    me
He delivereth me from mine enemies
Thou liftest me up above those that rise up against me
Thou hast delivered me from the violent man
Therefore will I give thanks unto thee O Lord among the
    heathen and sing praises unto thy name
The Lord Is My Protector

YESHUA IS COMING

Shout and behold Yeshua is coming
There will be signs in sun and moon and stars
On the earth distress of nations in perplexity because of the
      roaring of the sea and the waves
People fainting with fear and with foreboding of what is
      coming on the world
For the powers of the heavens will be shaken
And then they will see the Son of Man coming in a cloud
      with power and great glory
Luke 21:25-27 (KJV)

A SIBLING'S LOVE

Who loves their brother and sister lives in the light
There is nothing in them to make them fall apart
This is how we know what love is
Jesus Christ laid down His life for us
We should lay down our lives for our brothers and sisters
Carry each other's burdens and in this way, you will fulfill
    the law of Christ
Love one another as Christ loves you
A sibling's love will never depart even if you're far away

ANGELS

As I leave home every day, I know that I am safe
God encamps around me heavenly host of angels
God says to me
See, I am sending an angel ahead of you to guard you along
      the way and to bring you to the place I have prepared

ANOTHER BEAUTIFUL DAY

Another beautiful day
A beautiful creation God made
The fresh breeze in the air
The beautiful sites of color
Smell of the new seasons coming in
Laughter in the air
Knowing today will be a great day
Nature is beautiful in every way

SHE'S SOMEBODY'S DAUGHTER

A daughter is God's way of saying, "I thought you could use
    a lifelong friend"
There is nothing ordinary about you
You are the daughter of the King and your story is
    significant
May our daughters be like graceful pillars carved to beautify
    a palace
For you are all daughters of God through faith in Christ
    Jesus
So, you are no longer a slave but God's daughter
Since you are His daughter
God has made you His heir

Michele Fowler

NO LONGER BOUND TO POVERTY

The Spirit of the Sovereign Lord is on me
The Lord has anointed me to proclaim good news to the
      poor
He has sent me to bind up the brokenhearted
To proclaim freedom for the captives and release from
      darkness for the prisoners
Keep falsehood and lies far from me
Give me neither poverty nor riches
Give me only my daily bread

CHOSEN

You are a chosen race
A royal priesthood
A holy nation
A people for God's own possession
That you may proclaim the excellencies of Him who has
        called you
Out of darkness into His marvelous light
Just as He chose us in Him before the foundation of the
        world
We would be holy and blameless before Him
For we are His workmanship created in Christ
We are more than a chosen creation

QUEEN ESTHER'S PRAYER

My Lord, You alone are our King
Help me, I am alone and I have no help but You
I am fasting prayer unto You
For I am taking my life in my hand
I anoint myself from head to toe
Give me the strength and guidance to walk in faith
For I am a Queen, I will do all works upon to You

PRAYER FOR MY MOTHER

To my mother, I pray that God grant you all your heart
     desires
May He bring in your home the beauty of God's love
May He grant you long life and wipe away every tear from
     your past

PRAYER FOR MY DAUGHTER

The Lord bless you to be like Sarah, Ruth, Rebecca, Esther,
      Leah, Deborah
May He clothed you with virtue and compassion
May the Lord grant you long life
May the Lord send you a husband that will care for you,
      protect you, and defend you all the days of your life
May He favor with you with happiness and peace

PRAYER FOR MY SON

May my son be strong and courageous and not fear
For it is You Lord, our God, who goes with him
You will never leave him or forsake him
May my son walk before You as King David walked
With integrity of heart and uprightness
Doing according to all that You have called him to do
May he be a man of Your word
May the content of Your Torah be imparted on the table of
     his heart

A MOTHER'S PRAYER

When I first laid eyes on you
I knew there was something great on the inside of you
My prayer is you will never turn away from the will of God
May the Lord bless you and keep you
May the Lord make His face to shine upon you and be
      gracious unto you
May the Lord lift up His countenance upon you and give
      you peace
May you be fruitful all the days of your life
May He prepare for you a holy wife and make you a holy
      husband
May you forget the pain of your past
In Yeshua's Name

OCEAN PEACE

As I sit at the ocean I feel at peace
I talk to my best friend that keeps me at ease
It's the beautiful waves and the sunset
I look up to Heaven to my beloved
We have beautiful conversations
He's my safe place
I sit and write all my prayers knowing my love will listen

I Am Royalty

I am a crown of beauty in the hand of the Lord
And a royal diadem in the hand of my God
Ye have not chosen me, but I have chosen you, and
      ordained you
That ye should go and bring forth fruit, and that your fruit
      should remain
You are a chosen vessel through the adopted love of Jesus
      Christ as sons and daughters

ABOUT THE AUTHOR

Michele Fowler is from Beaumont, Texas. She is a 21-year-old mother and college student. Her passions are writing and serving the community. She is a Christian counselor, coaching the youth and inspiring hurt women around the world. Michele prays the poems will encourage, uplift and strengthen each one who reads *My Love Letter to God.*